discover countries

Pakistan

Geoff Barker

WAYLAND

First published in 2010 by Wayland
Copyright Wayland 2010

Wayland
Hachette Children's Books
338 Euston Road
London NW1 3BH

Wayland Australia
Level 17/207 Kent Street,
Sydney, NSW 2000

Concept design: Jason Billin
Editor: Susan Crean
Designer: Amy Sparks
Consultants: Rob Bowden and David Rogers

Produced for Wayland by
White-Thomson Publishing Ltd

www.wtpub.co.uk
+44 (0)845 362 8240

British Library Cataloguing in Publication Data

Barker, Geoff
Pakistan. - (Discover countries)
1. Pakistan - Geography - Juvenile literature
I. Title
914.3

ISBN-13: 9780750259811

Printed in Malaysia
Wayland is a division of Hachette Children's Books
an Hachette UK company
www.hachette.co.uk

All data in this book was researched in 2009
and has been collected from the latest sources available at that time.

Picture credits

1, Corbis/Mike Finn-Kelcey/Reuters; 3 (top), Dreamstime/Crazyeyedeas; 3 (bottom), Shutterstock/Zotyesz; 4 (map), Stefan Chabluk;
5, Corbis/Ed Kashi; 6, iStock/Wojciech Zwierzynski; 7, UN Images/Evan Schneider; 8, UN Images/Luke Powell; 9, Corbis/Tom Pietrasik;
10, iStock/Danish Khan; 11, Corbis/Ed Kashi; 12, Photoshot/Eye Ubiquitous; 13, Corbis/Charles & Josette Lenars; 14, Corbis/Christophe Boisvieux;
15, Corbis/MK Chaudhry/eps; 16, Corbis; 17, Photoshot/UPPA; 18, Corbis/Rahat Dar/epa; 19, Corbis/Ed Kashi; 20, Dreamstime/Zotyesz;
21, Corbis/Ed Kashi; 22, Dreamstime/Crazyeydeas; 23, Photoshot; 24, iStock/Danish Khan; 25, Shutterstock/Zotyesz;
26, Corbis/Mike Finn-Kelcey/Reuters; 27, Corbis/Galen Rowell; 28, Corbis/Christine Osborne; 29, Photoshot/NHPA
Cover images, Gonzalo Azumendi/Photolibrary (left), iStock/Danish Khan (right)

Contents

Discovering Pakistan

Pakistan has a rich history and today has one of the world's largest Muslim populations. With an area of more than 800,000 sq km (309,000 sq miles), the country is more than three times the size of the United Kingdom.

Early history

The central region of Pakistan was home to some of the world's earliest settlements. The Indus Valley Civilisation existed over four thousand years ago in the region where Punjab is today. From the sixteenth century, Pakistan was part of the once-powerful Mughal Empire. The empire gradually weakened and in the middle of the nineteenth century, the British took control of a large part of Asia that included Pakistan. The whole region controlled by Britain was known as British India.

A new country

Indian Muslims, mostly living in the north-west and east of British India, wanted their own homeland. In 1947, British India was divided up in a process called Partition. The Islamic Republic of Pakistan was formed for the Muslim population. The republic had two parts: East Pakistan and West Pakistan.

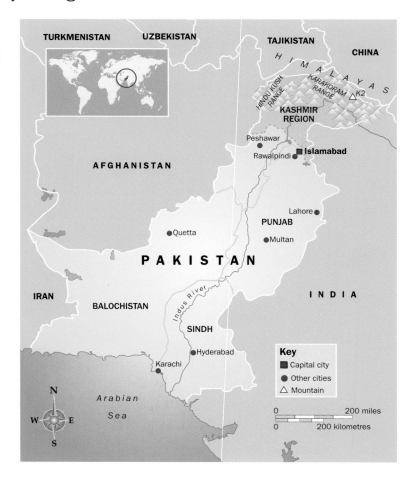

4

Wars with India

Pakistan and India went to war in 1947-8 and again in 1965. Both countries wanted to control the northern territory of Kashmir. Today Pakistan controls north-western Kashmir while India controls southern and south-eastern parts and China the easternmost parts.

Another war took place in 1971. People living in East Pakistan wanted independence from West Pakistan. The new nation of Bangladesh was created. West Pakistan became simply 'Pakistan'.

Government

In recent years, Pakistan has had different types of government. There have been military governments as well as civilian governments elected by the people. After more than eight years of military rule, Pakistan returned to civilian government in 2008.

One of the biggest threats to the current government is that of militant extremists. Some extreme groups are prepared to set off bombs to unsettle Pakistan's government. In 2009, Prime Minister Yusuf Raza Gilani vowed to stop terrorists in Pakistan.

Modern Pakistan

Pakistan is a fascinating, vibrant country with a unique culture. It is a blend of old traditions and modern influences. It has a rich mix of different peoples, modern cities and traditional villages and a wide variety of foods, arts and crafts.

 The Badshahi Mosque in Lahore is one of the largest mosques in the world. The courtyard can hold about 100,000 Muslim worshippers.

Pakistan Statistics

Area: 803,940 sq km (310,403 sq miles)

Capital city: Islamabad

Government type: Federal republic

Bordering countries: Afghanistan, China, India, Iran

Currency: Rupee

Language: Punjabi 48%, Sindhi 12%, Siraiki (a Punjabi variant) 10%, Pashtu 8%, Urdu (official) 8%, Balochi 3%, Hindko 2%, Brahui 1%, English, Burushaski and other 8%

Landscape and climate

Pakistan has varied landscapes. It has a 1,046-km (650-mile) humid coastline on the Arabian Sea. It also has towering, cold mountains in the north and north-west.

Landscape features

The Karakoram Range is a mountain range in Baltistan. This region in northern Pakistan is located near the border of China. The range is home to K2, the highest point in Pakistan and the second-highest in the world. It measures 8,611 m (28,251 ft) high.

Further to the west is another famous mountain range, the Hindu Kush. This range forms a natural border between Pakistan and the countries of Afghanistan and Tajikistan. The ranges are snow-capped, but the nearby valleys are very dry, with little rain or snow.

⬤ The Karakoram range forms the border between Pakistan and China.

DID YOU KNOW?
The world's second-highest mountain was measured in 1856. It was given the unusual name of K2 as it was the second peak to be measured in the Karakoram mountain range.

The Indus River

The great Indus River winds its way south through the centre of the country. The river originates in the Tibetan plateau, north of Pakistan. Water from the Indus irrigates the land of Punjab and the more southerly province of Sindh. The Indus floods every summer, bringing silt and fresh minerals to the fertile riverbanks. The floodwaters fill nearby lakes and marshes with much-needed water.

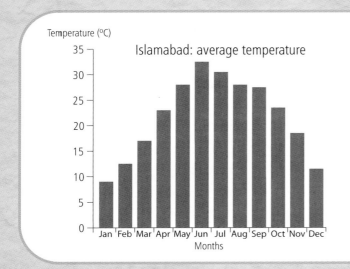

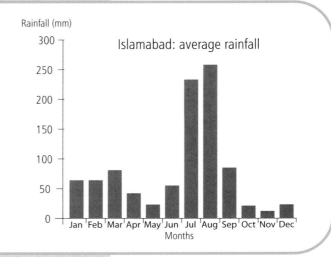

Climate variations

Much of Pakistan is hot, dry desert with little rainfall. However, the mountains of northern Pakistan are covered in snow. Settlements near the mountains have cold, often freezing winters, but dry, hot summers. The land along the Arabian Sea in the south-west corner of Pakistan has humid, temperate weather.

Great disasters

Earthquakes are quite frequent in Pakistan. The country has had three major earthquakes since 1974. In Pakistan's North West Frontier Province, a huge earthquake struck in October 2005. It was one of the world's deadliest earthquakes. The epicentre of the earthquake was the town of Balakot, but many other towns and villages across the province and Kashmir were affected, too. It killed around 70,000 people in Pakistan.

▶ Following a major earthquake in 2005, people searched through the rubble of a school in Balakot to find survivors.

Facts at a glance

Land area: 778,720 sq km (300,665 sq miles)

Water area: 25,220 sq km (9,737 sq miles)

Highest point: K2 (Mount Godwin-Austen) 8,611 m (28,251 ft)

Lowest point: Arabian Sea 0 m (0 ft)

Longest river: Indus River 2,900 km (1,800 miles)

Coastline: 1,046km (650 miles)

Population and health

In 1947, during Partition, huge numbers of people moved around the Indian subcontinent. At the time, eight million Muslims moved from India to the Islamic state of Pakistan. Today Pakistan is the sixth-most populated country in the world (behind China, India, the USA, Indonesia and Brazil).

In search of a better life

Many Afghan refugees have come to live in Pakistan. Afghans first fled to Pakistan in 1980, after Russia invaded Afghanistan late in 1979. Millions more fled further conflict in their home country during the last decade. Many of them live in refugee camps.

Facts at a glance

Total population: 176.2 million

Life expectancy at birth: 64.5 years

Children dying before the age of five: 10%

Ethnic composition: Punjabi 45%, Pashtun (Pathan) 15%, Sindhi 14%, Sariaki 8%, Muhajirs 8%, Balochi 4%, other 6%

▽ More than two million Afghan refugees live in Pakistan. Many refugees in Pakistan are children and young people.

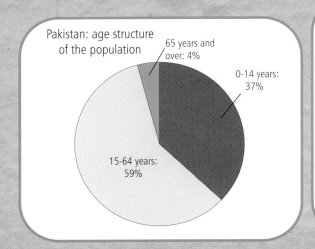

Pakistan: age structure of the population

- 65 years and over: 4%
- 0-14 years: 37%
- 15-64 years: 59%

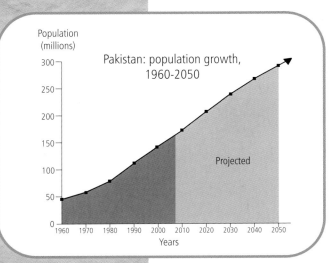

Population (millions)

Pakistan: population growth, 1960-2050

Projected

Years

Ethnic make-up

Most Pakistanis can trace their roots back to ancestors who also lived in the region. Nearly half of the population are Punjabis. Most Punjabis are descended from people originating from regions that are now the countries of Iran, Afghanistan and India. Sometimes the mix of different groups of people in the same city causes unrest and problems. For example, in Karachi Muslims with different beliefs, known as Sunni and Shia Muslims, sometimes clash.

Disease and death

Many people in Pakistan do not receive modern health care. The biggest danger to people in Pakistan is infectious diseases. These are passed on through infected food and water. Places without safe drinking water in city slum areas are most at risk. Half of all city people live in this type of shanty-town housing. Two of the biggest killers in Pakistan are malaria and tuberculosis.

DID YOU KNOW? Pakistan's population is increasing by 3.5 million people every year. This figure is about half a million more people than the total population of Wales!

Former Pakistan cricketer and politician Imran Khan established the Shaukat Khanum Memorial Hospital in Lahore in 1994. The hospital treats patients with cancer.

Settlements and living

Pakistan's largest settlements are found in coastal and agricultural areas. One of those areas is Punjab. Other regions, such as the deserts and mountains of Balochistan in the south-west, have a very small, scattered population.

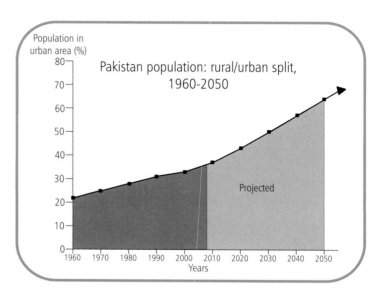

Pakistan population: rural/urban split, 1960-2050

Population in urban area (%)

Projected

Years

Punjab

The Punjab region stretches from Sindh in the south to Islamabad in the north. Over half of Pakistan's population live in Punjab, mostly in and around the cities of Islamabad, Rawalpindi and Lahore, in the north-east. Lahore is Punjab's largest city, with a population of about ten million. It is an ancient city with newer industrial areas.

Sprawling city

The coastal city of Karachi is located in Sindh province in southern Pakistan. In 1947, only 400,000 people lived there. Today, Karachi is the country's largest city, with a population of more than 12 million. Millions of Muslim refugees from India arrived in the city during Partition.

▽ Thousands of people live in low-income areas of Karachi, filled with multi-storey homes.

⬥ A woman collects water from a well in a village in the Cholistan Desert in Punjab. Many people living in the desert move from place to place in search of water.

Villages

Pakistan has many small villages. Most people in villages are farmers or labourers and their homes are often quite basic. They are usually single-storey buildings with a few rooms shared by a large family. Houses in villages are made from local materials, such as a mixture of clay and straw.

Types of housing

Only 40 per cent of Pakistan's houses are *pukka*, which means they are built of stone, brick, cement or concrete. Wealthy people live in these types of buildings. Poor people live in clay houses, which are not as expensive.

As the population continues to grow, there is an increasing shortage of houses in Pakistan. This results in huge slum areas in Pakistan's cities. Half of all Pakistan's city people live in *katchi abadis*, or shanty-town housing. Slum houses are usually roughly built from corrugated metal, plastic, reeds or other available materials.

DID YOU KNOW?

The province of Balochistan covers nearly half of Pakistan. Less than 7 per cent of the country's population live in this huge region because it is very dry and mountainous.

Family life

In Pakistan, traditions and customs are largely influenced by the religion of Islam. An important part of this has always been the family. Children often live with their parents, grandparents and even their great-grandparents. The father or the eldest male has the complete respect of the rest of the family.

Roles in a family

Women in a household are usually responsible for bringing up the children and doing the housework. In rural regions, many women work in the fields, because they need to make enough money to feed the family. If both parents work outside the home, then grandparents often help to look after young children.

▼ Three generations of a family often live under the same roof.

Various lifestyles

In many of Pakistan's small villages people continue to live in the same way that their parents and grandparents did. For example, fewer girls go to school and women dress and behave modestly in public.

In the larger cities, many people have begun to adopt more Western customs. They live in a more modern way. Girls are more likely to be educated, and young people in cities often wear Western-style clothing or have fashionable haircuts.

Muslim marriages

Muslim marriages are traditionally arranged between families. Marriages are often based on close family friendships. Pakistani families believe that traditional family links make a marriage more likely to succeed than freely choosing a partner. On average, men living in Pakistan get married when they are 23. Women get married at about the age of 20.

DID YOU KNOW? Many women, especially in rural Pakistan, wear a *burqa*. The *burqa* consists of a loose outer cloth, worn over the top of normal clothes. It has a head-covering and usually a veil to hide the face.

◄ Pakistani Muslims often wear colourful, traditional clothes on their wedding day. This Muslim couple is getting married in Karachi.

Religion and beliefs

Almost everyone in Pakistan follows the religion of Islam. Pakistan has the second-largest Muslim population in the world, after Indonesia. There are also small groups of Hindus, Christians and Sikhs.

Two branches of Islam

The religion of Islam was founded by the Prophet Muhammad at the beginning of the seventh century. Muslims have one god, called Allah. Islam has two main branches – there are Sunni Muslims and Shia Muslims. In Pakistan, there are about 128 million Sunni Muslims. There are 34 million Shia Muslims.

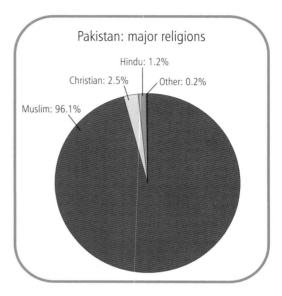

Pakistan: major religions

Hindu: 1.2%
Christian: 2.5%
Other: 0.2%
Muslim: 96.1%

▼ A group of boys study the Qur'an at the Wazir Khan Mosque in Lahore.

An Islamic nation

The country's full title is the Islamic Republic of Pakistan. Islam is Pakistan's major religion. Muslim families get up at sunrise when they hear the call to prayer from their local mosque. They pray four more times during the day.

Religious dates

Ramadan is the holiest month in the Islamic calendar. Muslims do not drink or eat from dawn to dusk for 30 days during Ramadan. Muslims celebrate the end of Ramadan with a special festival called Eid ul-Fitr. After Eid prayers, people often visit the graves of family members. Here they pray for dead relatives. Muslims in Pakistan celebrate the end of fasting with *savayya*. This is a special dish of thin, toasted noodles, served for the first breakfast after the fast.

Other beliefs

Sufism is an ancient mystical version of Islam. Some people, called Sufis or 'dervishes', still follow Sufism in Pakistan, although its practice has declined. Some mountain people of northern Pakistan believe in shamanism, or the belief that a soul or spirit lives in every single object.

▼ Pakistani girls decorate their hands and wrists with henna dye. They are preparing for the Muslim festival Eid-ul-Fitr that marks the end of a holy period of fasting, called Ramadan.

DID YOU KNOW?
Sufism is perhaps most famous for its spectacular dancing dervishes and singing of mystical poetry, or *qawwali*. The whirling dance is used by Sufi followers to go into a trance and achieve inner peace.

Education and learning

In 1947, the newly independent country of Pakistan had few schools. As a result, the population was poorly educated. Education has since improved, but Pakistan's levels of literacy are still low compared to other countries in the world.

Literacy

In Pakistan today, only half of the population is literate. A young man is more likely to be literate than a young woman – 63 per cent compared to only 36 per cent of women. By the end of the twentieth century, only 15 per cent of young Pakistanis were receiving secondary education.

⏷ In this school the boys are taking part in physical education while the girls watch in the background.

A mere 10 per cent were receiving a primary education. Pakistan had a severe shortage of schools, especially in rural areas. Some schools had very few resources. They did not have enough trained teachers or classroom materials. The government has increased teacher training, and there has been a steady improvement. Literacy has increased from 40 to 50 per cent in the past 10 years.

Further education

In 1947, West Pakistan had only one university, the University of the Punjab. Now there are many public and private universities, most of them in the major cities of Islamabad, Lahore, Karachi, Peshawar and Rawalpindi.

Even for those who do get degrees, job prospects can be poor in Pakistan. Over the years, many trained people have looked for opportunities in foreign countries and have emigrated, mainly to Saudi Arabia, the UK and the USA.

▼ Female students in Karachi graduate from university. The literacy rate for urban women is over five times that of rural women.

DID YOU KNOW?

The University of the Punjab in Lahore was established in 1882. It was the fourth university to be established by the British colonial authorities on the Indian subcontinent – after those at Mumbai, Kolkata and Madras in India.

Employment and economy

Pakistan is a growing, developing country with a huge workforce. Compared to developed Western countries, these people are paid very little. Pakistan is trying to use its resources to improve its economy and wealth, but the country is also looking for more help from foreign countries.

Economy

In recent years, fuel prices have increased all over the world. Pakistan buys more than two-thirds of the oil it uses from other countries. This has made fuel more expensive as well as products made from oil, from shampoos to candles. Ordinary people have become poorer. Their money does not buy as much as it did.

However, Pakistan has increased production of the goods it makes. Major products include cotton textiles, cement, paper, fertilizers and other chemicals. This increase can begin to improve Pakistan's money problems, as it has big debts to other countries.

People and jobs

In Pakistan, there is a labour force of slightly over 50 million people. This is the number of people able to work. About 43 per cent of them, or well over 20 million people, work in agriculture.

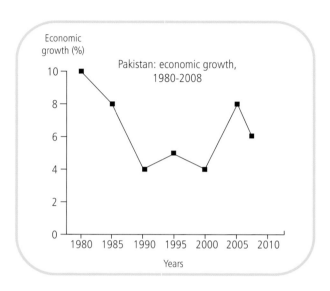

▼ Young apprentices learn practical skills on the job to earn a living. Here, a mechanic in Peshawar in northern Pakistan welds a metal plate in a car repair shop.

The remainder work in industry (20 per cent) and services (37 per cent) such as banks, schools, hospitals and transport.

Unemployment was 7.4 per cent in 2008 in Pakistan and the figure continues to rise. Added to this many people are 'underemployed'. This means that they are in very low-paid jobs, or that they would like to work more, but can only find part-time work.

Some employers and businesses use children to make products such as carpets and sports goods. This sort of child labour is against the law. Out of a total 40 million children aged 5 to 14 in Pakistan, 4 million of them are working.

Working women

Much of Pakistan's agricultural work is done by women. They also care for their children. In the past, Pakistani women worked in only a few jobs apart from agriculture, such as teaching in girls' schools or nursing.

In Pakistan's government there are female MPs, and many professional women work in Pakistan's cities as doctors, professors, lawyers, bankers and business women. But overall, most Pakistani women continue to lead traditional lives, looking after their children as well as working.

▶ Women meet in the home of a Hunza family in northern Pakistan. Through women's organisations like this, local women own orchards and livestock.

DID YOU KNOW?
Benazir Bhutto became the first female Prime Minister of Pakistan in 1988. This event showed how far women had come in the country. She became the first-ever woman head of a Muslim state.

Industry and trade

Pakistan has many natural resources, such as oil and gas. The country produces important exports such as textiles and leather goods.

Manufacturing

During Pakistan's early years of independence, Karachi was the country's centre of manufacturing. However, during the 1970s, Lahore and the nearby cities in the north-east began to grow in size. Clothing, food processing and medicines are all produced in this region. Pakistan also exports sporting goods, carpets and rugs.

DID YOU KNOW?
The Tarbela Dam, crossing the River Indus near Islamabad, is the world's largest dam made of earth. It stores freshwater for drinking and irrigation. It also makes electricity.

▶ Pakistan is rich in natural gas reserves. This drilling rig in northern Pakistan is used to drill under the surface of the Earth to reach the gas.

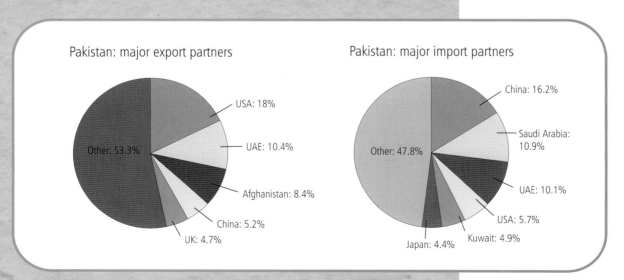

Manufacturing accounts for about one fifth of the country's Gross Domestic Product (GDP). GDP is the total value of all goods and services in one year.

Mining

Pakistan has about 20 different types of minerals. It mines coal and iron ore as well as copper, rock salt, limestone and gypsum. Limestone and gypsum are used to make cement.

Pakistan has oil reserves and produces 68,670 barrels (of 159 litres) per day. The country uses 345,000 barrels a day, so demand is much greater than supply. Pakistan also has large reserves of natural gas. It uses as much natural gas as it produces.

⬤ About 85 per cent of the world's footballs are made in Sialkot, in north-eastern Punjab. Here Pakistani workers test the air pressure of the inner football tubes.

Pakistan: major export partners

USA: 18%
UAE: 10.4%
Other: 53.3%
Afghanistan: 8.4%
China: 5.2%
UK: 4.7%

Pakistan: major import partners

China: 16.2%
Saudi Arabia: 10.9%
Other: 47.8%
UAE: 10.1%
USA: 5.7%
Kuwait: 4.9%
Japan: 4.4%

Farming and food

Most of Pakistan is hot and dry and does not get enough rainfall for crops. However, there is fertile land around the Indus River and its tributaries. People in this region irrigate their land with water from the Indus River.

Farming

Most farmers in Pakistan use traditional farming tools and methods. For example, they work in fields using ploughs pulled by animals. The amount of tractors used on the land is increasing though. Other labour-saving types of machinery, such as crop threshers, are also used.

Facts at a glance

Farmland: 26% of total land area

Main agricultural exports: rice, oils

Main agricultural imports: palm oil, tea

Average daily calorie intake: 2,340 calories

Raising sheep is a way of life for many rural families in Pakistan. Pakistan ranks eighth in the world for the number of sheep it has.

Pakistan's major food crop is wheat. Other cereal crops include rice, millet, sorghum, corn and barley. Most of this produce is to feed the Pakistani population, but rice is a vital export product. Farmers also grow vegetables and fruits such as apples, bananas and melons. Other farms produce milk, beef, mutton and eggs.

Fishing

Fishers from the city of Karachi and Pakistan's coastal regions use trawlers to catch fresh seafood and fish such as lobsters, prawns and pomfret. Rice and fish is a favourite dish of people living along the banks of the Indus River in the southern province of Sindh.

Food

A meal in Pakistan usually includes bread, rice and vegetables. If a family can afford it, meat or poultry is added. *Biryani* is a popular dish, consisting of rice cooked in a meat sauce. *Chapattis* are flat, round breads, used to mop up the tasty sauces. Every region or province has its own special dishes. For example, Punjab is famous for its different types of lentil dishes, or *dhal*.

▶ Workers unload fish from a boat in Karachi. About 90 per cent of the fish coming into Pakistan goes through Karachi Fish Harbour.

Transport and communications

People travel around Pakistan in many different ways. In country areas, many people still use animal-drawn carts. Pakistan's big cities have the same traffic problems as any other – they are full of vehicles that pollute the air.

City travel

Roads in major cities are often full to bursting with taxis, cars, trucks, buses and bicycles. The use of three-wheel taxis, or auto-rickshaws, has been restricted in many cities. This is because of the air pollution they cause.

> **Facts at a glance**
>
> **Total roads:** 259,758 km (161,406 miles)
> **Paved roads:** 162,879 km (101,208 miles)
> **Railways:** 8,163 km (5,072 miles)
> **Major airports:** 35
> **Major ports:** 2

▼ Oil containers travel by train from Cantt Station in Karachi. Slum dwellings are right next to the side of the rail tracks.

Travelling further afield

For longer journeys around the country, Pakistan has more than 8,000 km (5,000 miles) of railways. However, many people travel and send goods longer distances by bus or by truck. As global links become more important, air transport of passengers and cargo has increased in recent years.

Communications

Pakistan does not provide main line telephone service to areas outside its cities. The number of main line phones has increased slightly over the past 10 years, but still only 4.5 million main lines are in use.

At the beginning of the century there were only 300,000 mobile phone users in Pakistan. Numbers have rocketed in recent years – and there are now more than 80 million mobile telephone users in the country.

○ Some Pakistani truck drivers customize their trucks for fun. They are beautifully decorated and make a colourful sight on the roads.

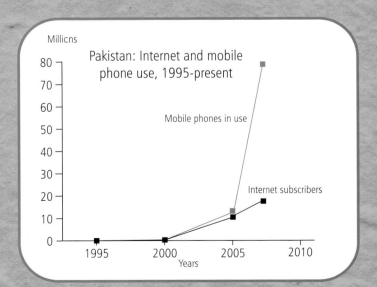

Millions

Pakistan: Internet and mobile phone use, 1995-present

Mobile phones in use

Internet subscribers

Years

DID YOU KNOW?

Pakistan is the world's largest user of compressed natural gas (CNG). This form of energy powers over two million natural gas vehicles in Pakistan. CNG cars are 'greener' than petrol cars.

Leisure and tourism

In a recent survey, most people in Pakistan claimed they have little free time, but spend it watching TV or with family and friends. Popular sports include hockey and cricket. Kite flying is also a favourite pastime.

Sport

Hockey is one of the most popular sports in Pakistan, and is an important part of the country's culture. Pakistan has won four World Cup titles in hockey, more than any other nation. But cricket is even more popular than hockey. Pakistan has sporting legends such as Imran Khan, who led Pakistan to victory in the Cricket World Cup in 1992.

⬤ Children enjoy playing cricket anywhere in Pakistan. These boys are playing on waste land in the city of Faisalabad using a pile of bricks as a wicket.

Leisure time

Both Pakistani children and adults love flying kites. Children also enjoy playing marbles and traditional board games such as ludo.

Most families in Pakistan have television sets. Soap operas and quiz shows are popular television programmes. With growing Internet access and computers, children enjoy computer games, too.

DID YOU KNOW?

On Basant Night, traditionally after the first day of spring, lovers of kite flying take to the streets of Basant in Punjab. Kite flyers race and duel in the night skies with the help of searchlights.

Getting together

Traditionally, at the end of the day, men meet to drink tea and play cards. Following Friday prayers, men often stay behind at their local mosque to chat with friends. When not looking after children, women might watch films and listen to music with friends.

After a hard day's work, people enjoy resting on a *charpois*, a traditional string bed. The end of the working day is often a social occasion when many people gather on city rooftops to talk and relax.

Tourism

Currently, there is a small tourist industry in Pakistan. Climbers and trekkers enjoy the country's majestic, great mountain ranges. There are many World Heritage sites such as Taxila, as well as forts, tombs, shrines and mosques. Most tourists travel from the United Kingdom, USA and Afghanistan. More than 40 per cent are from the UK. Most foreign tourists visit the popular province of Punjab. Karimabad in the Hunza valley is another of Pakistan's many highlights.

🔻 Hikers trek in Pakistan's Karakoram Range. Although the mountains are remote, the Karakoram Highway passes through villages such as Passu, where hikers can start or take a break on their walks.

Environment and wildlife

Pakistan has a range of different habitats for plant and animal wildlife – from the rare Indus River dolphin to more common jackals, foxes and wild cats. But today there are more and more pressures on Pakistan's environment and varied wildlife.

Environmental problems

Because much of Pakistan is dry, water is a key issue in the country. Pakistan has limited natural freshwater resources. Most of the population does not have access to clean drinking water.

Pakistan's deserts are growing due to climate change. Other environmental problems include pollution, especially in the major cities, and deforestation caused by the illegal felling of trees.

Facts at a glance

Proportion of area protected: 9.2%

Biodiversity (known species): 5,718

Threatened species: 50

▼ The Tarbela Dam is a massive structure 150 metres (500 ft) high, on the Indus River in northern Pakistan.

Water habitats

Many aquatic birds such as mallards, teals, geese and spoonbills can be seen in the country's lakes. The Indus River delta is home to crocodiles, pythons and wild boars.

Water pollution, dams and hunting have all endangered the survival of the Indus River dolphin. The World Wildlife Fund in Pakistan has worked to conserve the country's unique and beautiful wildlife. Indus River dolphin numbers have recovered from a low of 150 to the current figure of about 1,000 dolphins.

Pakistan's wildlife

In some parts of Pakistan there is rich and varied wildlife. Pakistan's large mammals include leopards, Siberian ibex, wild sheep, Chiltan wild goats and Himalayan bears. Habitat destruction and hunting have reduced numbers of some species of Pakistan's wildlife. Snow leopards and Chiltan wild goats have become very rare.

⚠ Snow leopards are an endangered species found in the Karakoram mountain range.

DID YOU KNOW?
The snow leopard is one of Pakistan's rarest mammals and is an endangered species. Across its entire range in the mountains of Asia, there are thought to be only 6,000 snow leopards left in the wild.

Glossary

ancestors people who were family members a long time ago

authority power or control

British India the Indian sub-continent which was ruled by Britain from the middle of the nineteenth century to the middle of the twentieth century

child labour making children do work

civilian government a government that is run by the people, rather than an army

climate the normal weather conditions of an area

deforestation the clearing of trees

emigrate to leave a country and go to live in another

employer someone who provides work for another

endangered species a type of animal or plant that is in danger of dying out

epicentre centre of an earthquake

ethnic belonging to a particular human group with common traditions and culture

exports goods or services that are sold to another country

freshwater inland water that is not salty

humid moist or damp

illegal against the law

imports goods or services that are brought in from another country

industry any activity that processes or manufactures raw materials into finished products

infected contaminated, or tainted, with germs

irrigate to supply land with water using ditches and canals

Islamic to do with the religion of Islam

malaria deadly disease spread by mosquitoes

militants people who aggressively support a cause

military government a government that is run by an army

mineral solid substance that is found in rocks or the ground; salt, gold and limestone are examples of minerals

Mughal Empire powerful Muslim empire (from early sixteenth century to mid-nineteenth century)

mystical to do with sacred beliefs

natural resources water, trees and minerals that are found naturally in an area

province region that is run, or governed, as a unit

Qur'an holy book of Islam

refugees people forced to leave their homes or country, usually because of fighting

reserves stocks, or materials available for future use

Shia one of the two main branches of Islam

silt sediment or bits of mud in a river or lake; when rivers flood, silt can help make the land more fertile

Sunni one of the two main branches of Islam

temperate having a mild climate

textiles cloth or fabric that is usually woven

thresher machine that threshes crops, to separate grain from husks

traffic congestion when too many vehicles use busy roads and there are often heavy traffic jams

tributary branch or offshoot of a river

tuberculosis infectious disease whose sufferers have bad cough and loss of weight

Topic web

Use this topic web to explore Pakistan themes in different areas of your curriculum.

Geography
Find Pakistan on an atlas or globe. It shares borders with Iran, India, China and one other country. What is its name? Which is the longest border? Find out the capitals of each of the four neighbouring countries.

History
Pakistan had three wars with India in the twentieth century. Find out some more about the conflicts. What is the relationship between the two countries like today?

Science
Pakistan mines many different types of minerals. Find out more about copper, limestone and gypsum. Are any of them metals? What are they used for?

English
Using the information in this book, write a short story about life in Pakistan. Imagine you are leaving your classroom at the end of a school day. Describe what you see and do as you travel home.

Pakistan

Maths
Pakistan's currency is the Pakistani rupee (PKR). Find out how many rupees there are in £1. Work out how much a loaf of bread and your favourite magazine would cost in rupees.

ICT
Imagine you are planning to visit Pakistan. Use the Internet to work out how you can fly to Karachi. What can you do when you get there? Make a list of five places you'd like to visit.

Design and Technology
Make a papier-mache model of a mud house. Find a picture online to use as a model. First, use chicken wire or other materials to make a frame. Then cover with papier-mache. Once it is dry, paint the house.

Citizenship
Find out what life was like in 1947 during Partition. Imagine you are a Muslim from India trying to get to Karachi in Pakistan. Write a letter about what you think it must have been like.

Further information and index

Further reading

Pakistan (Country File), Ian Graham (Franklin Watts 2005)
Pakistan (Insight Guide) (APA Publications Pte Ltd 2007)

Web

https://www.cia.gov/library/publications/the-world-factbook/geos/pk.html
Key statistics about the landscape, population, economy, government and more.
http://news.bbc.co.uk/1/hi/world/south_asia/country_profiles/1157960.stm
Country profile on Pakistan with key facts and links to other Pakistan websites.
http://www.tourism.gov.pk/
Official tourist website for Pakistan with lots of interesting information on destinations as well as fairs and festivals.

Index